DOGS AT WORK

HERDING DOGS

BY MARIE PEARSON

WWW.APEXEDITIONS.COM

Copyright © 2023 by Apex Editions, Mendota Heights, MN 55120. All rights reserved. No part of this book may be reproduced or utilized in any form or by any means without written permission from the publisher.

Apex is distributed by North Star Editions:
sales@northstareditions.com | 888-417-0195

Produced for Apex by Red Line Editorial.

Photographs ©: Shutterstock Images, cover, 1, 4–5, 6–7, 8–9, 10–11, 12–13, 14, 15, 16–17, 20, 21, 22–23, 24–25, 26–27, 27, 29; iStockphoto, 18–19

Library of Congress Control Number: 2022912276

ISBN
978-1-63738-422-0 (hardcover)
978-1-63738-449-7 (paperback)
978-1-63738-502-9 (ebook pdf)
978-1-63738-476-3 (hosted ebook)

Printed in the United States of America
Mankato, MN
012023

NOTE TO PARENTS AND EDUCATORS

Apex books are designed to build literacy skills in striving readers. Exciting, high-interest content attracts and holds readers' attention. The text is carefully leveled to allow students to achieve success quickly. Additional features, such as bolded glossary words for difficult terms, help build comprehension.

TABLE OF CONTENTS

CHAPTER 1
A FARMER'S HELPER 4

CHAPTER 2
MOVING ANIMALS 10

CHAPTER 3
TYPES OF HERDING 16

CHAPTER 4
TRAINING 22

COMPREHENSION QUESTIONS • 28
GLOSSARY • 30
TO LEARN MORE • 31
ABOUT THE AUTHOR • 31
INDEX • 32

CHAPTER 1

A FARMER'S HELPER

A farmer wants to bring his cows into the barn. But they are at the other side of a hill. So, he calls his border collie.

Border collies are known for being smart and working hard.

Herding dogs must obey commands, even when they are far from their owners.

The farmer says, "Away!" His dog runs over the hill. She can't see or hear the farmer now. She finds the cows.

HERDING COMMANDS

Away is a common herding command. It tells the dog to circle the herd counterclockwise. Another command is *come-bye*. It means to go clockwise around the herd.

Herding dogs make sure all the animals arrive safely.

FAST FACT

Border collies and Australian shepherds are both common **breeds** of herding dogs.

8

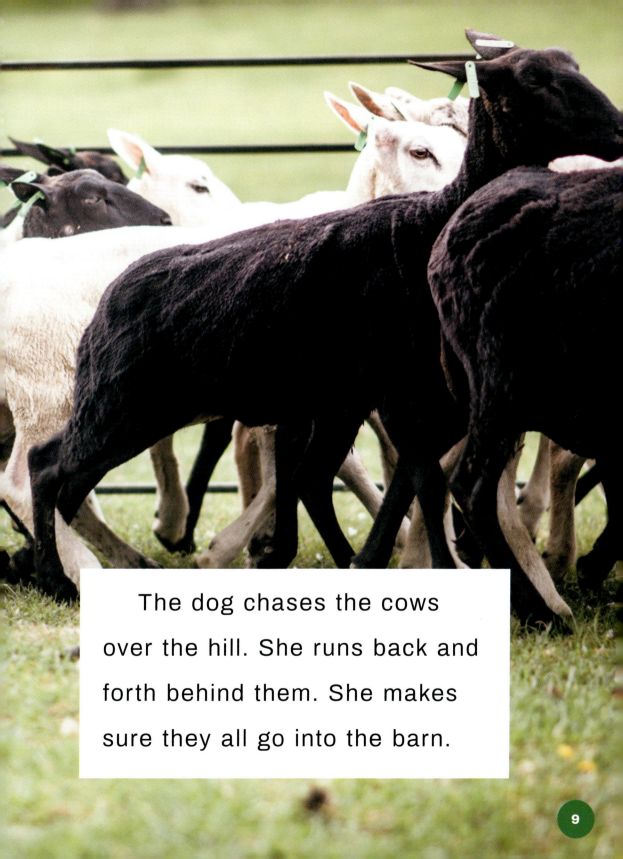

The dog chases the cows over the hill. She runs back and forth behind them. She makes sure they all go into the barn.

CHAPTER 2

MOVING ANIMALS

Herding dogs work with **livestock**. They move the animals from one place to another.

Herding dogs often help farmers move animals to new pens or fields.

One dog can move a large group of animals.

Herding dogs often keep the livestock in a group. They get all the animals to go the same way. And they make sure none are left behind.

FAST FACT

People have used herding dogs for hundreds of years or more.

Dogs may bring sheep to farmers for shearing or tagging.

Herding dogs may also move one animal at a time. The dog guides the animal toward a person or a pen. There, people can take care of it.

HERDING DOG TRAITS

Herding is hard work. Dogs must be smart, fast, and strong. Dogs often work on ground that is steep or muddy. They must pay attention to their surroundings to stay safe.

Some dogs help farmers bring in sheep from steep hills or mountains.

CHAPTER 3

TYPES OF HERDING

Dogs can herd in several ways. Some are tending dogs. They move in circles around a herd. They keep the animals in one area.

Some herding dogs make sure animals stay together in one place.

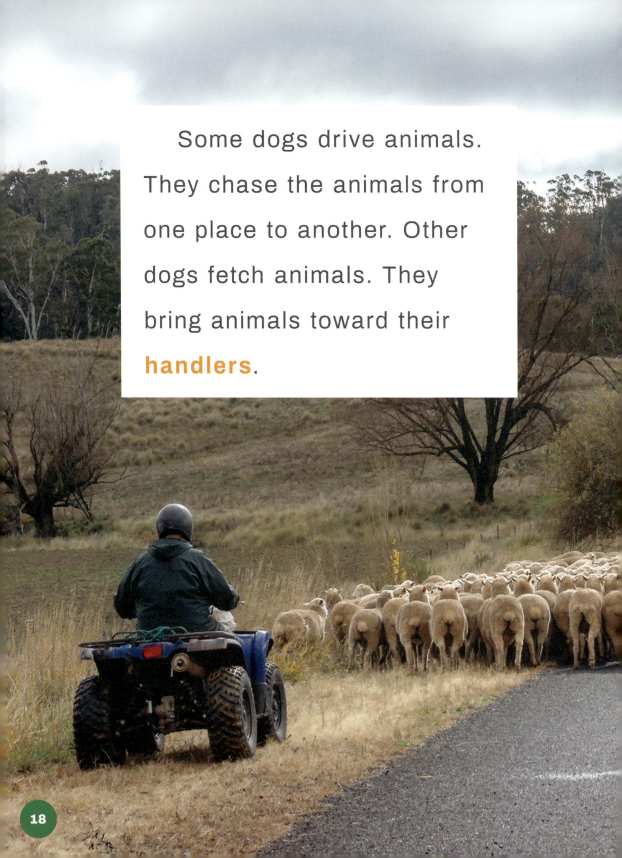

Some dogs drive animals. They chase the animals from one place to another. Other dogs fetch animals. They bring animals toward their **handlers**.

FAST FACT
Dogs can herd several types of animals. These include cows, sheep, goats, ducks, and pigs.

Two or three dogs may work together to drive a group of animals.

19

To move livestock, dogs might **crouch** and stare. Dogs may also bark. Some nip at the animals' heels.

Border collies often crouch low when they herd. They use their eyes to hurry the animals, too.

> Some dogs bump or nip animals to guide them.

HERDING HISTORY

Dogs are descended from wolves. Wolves use circling and nipping to separate an animal from its herd. People bred herding dogs to use these skills without killing the livestock.

CHAPTER 4

TRAINING

Herding dogs must be taught many commands. Dogs can learn to herd at any age. But it's easiest to train puppies.

Handlers train dogs to obey words and hand signals.

Trainers start with basic commands. Then, they teach dogs harder skills.

First, dogs learn to lie down and stay. Dogs must always come when called. And they need to obey quickly.

FAST FACT
Some dogs will naturally herd animals at just a few weeks old.

The best dogs at herding trials win prizes.

After that, dogs learn specific herding skills. They practice with animals. Handlers make training easy and fun. That way, dogs are happy to keep learning new commands.

Some herding dogs learn as many as 60 commands.

HERDING TRIALS

Some people do herding trials with their dogs. These events test the dogs' skills. Dogs take turns moving livestock in a fenced area. Judges watch and give them a score.

COMPREHENSION QUESTIONS

Write your answers on a separate piece of paper.

1. Write a few sentences about the ways dogs herd livestock.

2. Would you like to try training a dog to compete in herding trials? Why or why not?

3. What task do tending dogs do?

   A. move animals toward a person
   B. move animals away from a person
   C. keep animals in one place

4. Why do herding dogs need to be strong?

   A. They need to chase people.
   B. They need to carry animals.
   C. They need to run many places.

5. What does **surroundings** mean in this book?

Dogs often work on ground that is steep or muddy. They must pay attention to their surroundings to stay safe.

    A. ways to find food
    B. things and spaces that are nearby
    C. different types of clothes

6. What does **obey** mean in this book?

Dogs must always come when called. And they need to obey quickly.

    A. do what is asked
    B. not do what is asked
    C. move very slowly

Answer key on page 32.

GLOSSARY

bred
Raised animals, often in a way that creates certain looks or abilities.

breeds
Specific types of dogs that have their own looks and abilities.

command
A way of telling a dog what to do.

counterclockwise
Moving in a circle in the opposite direction that the hands on a clock move.

crouch
To bend down and stay close to the ground.

descended
Related to a person or animal that lived long ago.

handlers
People who work with and train animals.

livestock
Animals kept and cared for by humans.

BOOKS

Davidson, B. Keith. *Herding Dog.* New York: Crabtree Publishing, 2022.

Furstinger, Nancy. *Herding Dogs*. Minneapolis: Abdo Publishing, 2019.

Green, Sara. *Herding Dogs*. Minneapolis: Bellwether Media, 2021.

ONLINE RESOURCES

Visit **www.apexeditions.com** to find links and resources related to this title.

ABOUT THE AUTHOR

Marie Pearson is an author and editor of books for young readers. Her first dog was an Australian shepherd who thought he could herd cats. She currently trains and competes with her standard poodle in multiple dog sports.

A
Australian shepherds, 8

B
bark, 20
barn, 4, 9
border collies, 4, 8

C
commands, 7, 22, 26
cows, 4, 6, 9, 19
crouch, 20

D
drive, 18

F
farmer, 4, 6

H
handlers, 18, 26
herding trials, 27

L
livestock, 10, 13, 16, 20–21, 27

N
nip, 20–21

P
pen, 14

T
tending dogs, 16
training, 22, 26

W
wolves, 21

ANSWER KEY:
1. Answers will vary; 2. Answers will vary; 3. C; 4. C; 5. B; 6. A